About Lisa Stice's *FORCES*

"In her word-experiments with the unseen forces at work in our lives—the pushes-and-pulls of parenting, the moments of quiet natures observed [...]—Lisa Stice captures an essential and modern magic."
— Randy Brown, author of *So Frag & So Bold*
and *Welcome to FOB Haiku: War Poems from Inside the Wire*

❖   ❖   ❖

"There is so much life in these poems—daily life, and overarching life. As with Sylvia Plath, Louis MacNeice, Natasha Trethewey and others, Stice brings visions of war and peace, violence and tenderness, into the sort of troublesome, necessary contact we should always keep them in."
— Andria Williams, author of *The Longest Night: A Novel*

❖   ❖   ❖

"Don't let the quiet moments fool you. Stice highlights [...] the spaces between our worries about the outside world, and the inner lives of our families. Her daughter inspires us to be strong when she says that her dog 'makes me braver.' Stice asks Sun Tzu to teach her to be 'serene and indestructible.' Her poetry shows that she learned how."
— Eric Chandler, author of *Kekekabic*
and *Hugging This Rock: Poems of Earth & Sky, Love & War*

❖   ❖   ❖

"The best poems in this collection are the ones that seem the simplest. The longer you wait after finishing them, the deeper they sink into your being—a seemingly effortless transportation into how the weight of being a military spouse can find its way into the everyday. In life, as in these poems, sometimes the silent spaces are the most powerful."
— Colin D. Halloran, author of *American Etiquette*,
Icarian Flux, and *Shortly Thereafter*

Other Military-themed Books from Middle West Press LLC

anthologies

Our Best War Stories:
Prize-winning Poetry & Prose
from the Col. Darron L. Wright Memorial Awards
Edited by Christopher Lyke

Why We Write:
Craft Essays on Writing War
Edited by Randy Brown
& Steve Leonard

Reporting for Duty:
U.S. Citizen-Soldier Journalism
from the Afghan Surge, 2010-2011
Edited by Randy Brown

❖ ❖ ❖

poetry collections

Hugging This Rock:
Poems of Earth & Sky, Love & War
by Eric Chandler

Permanent Change of Station and *Forces*
by Lisa Stice

Welcome to FOB Haiku:
War Poetry from Inside the Wire,
by Randy Brown, a.k.a. "Charlie Sherpa"

FORCES

Poems by
Lisa Stice

Middle West Press LLC
Johnston, Iowa

❖   ❖   ❖

Poetry / Military Life / Family & War

Forces: Poems by Lisa Stice
ISBN (print): 978-1-953665-00-3
ISBN (e-book): 978-1-953665-03-4
Library of Congress Control Number: 2021917915

❖   ❖   ❖

Middle West Press LLC
P.O. Box 1153
Johnston, Iowa 50131-9420
www.middlewestpress.com

❖   ❖   ❖

*Special thanks to James Burns of Aurora, Colorado
and Aramis Calderon of Safety Harbor, Florida
Your patronage helps publish great military-themed writing!*
www.aimingcircle.com

❖   ❖   ❖

Cover images: Portion of "Woman Holding a Balance" (1664)
by Johannes Vermeer (1632-1675)

U.S. Marine Corps photo (2011) by Lance Cpl. Kyle McNally,
Marine Forces Special Operations Command (MARSOC)

Author photo by Andria Williams

For Saoirse and Seamus

CONTENTS

OPERATIONAL

GRAVITATIONAL

DEFENSIVE

FRICTIONAL

TENSILE

MAGNETIC

NOTES

Operational

Ritual Hunts

Here we have a vessel,
hollowed out and empty
and we squirm in the need
to fill it with wooden apples,
potpourri or junk mail
we will throw away months
from now. Ritual shines
above our design as we crowd
our heads with words, turn
pages in a right to left manner,
read in a left to right manner,
enrich our lives away
and still wait for an established
secret somewhere between lines.
How we always
place the car keys here,
hang the dog's leash near
the door, turn the lights out
at bedtime.

Operator

For now, he supervises pretend wars.
I imagine the game played by children
where when they fall, their arms lay
across their eyes, and they can't move
until a friend taps their hands, then they
are to their feet as if nothing happened.

Still, there is little I really know:
entering and exiting facades, making
sure students do what is right (whatever
that is) and not compromise themselves
or anyone else. And I know it means
traveling on the road or in the air
to some place that isn't here.

I ask if they use real bullets, but of
course he can't tell me that, and
there is all that other ammunition
I know the names of but don't like
to talk about and all the kinds that
I don't know the names of and would
prefer it to remain that way.

Counting the Casualties
after the KC-130 incident July 10, 2017

my husband asks if I heard the news
and I say yes

we are quiet for a long while

then I ask if he knew any of them
and he says yes

I am home
he is home
our daughter plays in the living room
our dog naps under the coffee table

Midlife

these days like snails
in the garden—multiplying—
dividing and conquering
leaf by leaf and petal by petal—

holes—empty spots
where spiders make their homes—
where larvae wait
to eat their fill before metamorphosis

these days like snails creep along
then one day number thousands—
and I ask *what happened*
when did time lose control

Work Trip

Saying goodbye with half-open eyes
fools me into believing later that
I could roll to my other side when
fully awake and see your face right
there—*have a safe flight*
muttered by rote in my dream

but our dog reminds me that you
aren't here to feed him. I share with
him a banana, a treat before I scoop
his kibble before we sit down
on the couch in a too-quiet house

before our daughter wakes to call
my name over and over until
I make my way to her door and open
it with our dog sliding through
and our daughter asking *where's Daddy.*

Ode to the Rotary Phone

There was a deliberateness
in you, a tracing of a path,
a doubling-back, then
a forging-forth again
with a new mission and
doubling-back again, circular
yet fixed, always returning
home to wait for the next
rotation with those
familiar ticks so close
they whirred, pulses
to signal a conversation
about to initiate, a rotation
to interrupt electrical currents
with an exchange of codes:
ten digits, ten pulses,
then I'd receive your *hello*:
scratchy and distant
(it seems now) as a trilobite
scuttling across the Cambrian era.

Devising the Strategy

to achieve the aim involves

communication: me saying *I am afraid*
and *I am worried* and *the dog just*
laid on the mat for hours because
you forgot to say goodbye to him
and *the car needs engine coolant*
and *don't forget I love you* and
you saying *I am also afraid* and
I won't forget to include him next
time and *it's on the bottom shelf*
on the left side of the garage and
I know and *don't forget I love you*

planning: losing hours of sleep
visualizing how I will safely
load and unload a girl and a dog
from the car in a parking lot
how I will fit in the tasks you
normally take care of: mowing,
weeding, small maintenance

adaptation: somehow it always
happens without me really thinking
I just wake earlier before the alarm
and sweep the floor or fold the laundry
yesterday left on the guest bed or
pull the trash and recycling to the curb
or check the tire pressure and the oil
on the car or catch some news with
the rest of the day moving forward
tasks completed with a utility of force

Rejoice, for

two Eastern Blue Birds have made their home
in the birdhouse my daughter painted and
my husband nailed to a tree—we watch
from the kitchen window, the pair, merry
in their find, grateful for this little shelter
decorated with a loving hand—the hope
of the young—my daughter says *there will be
eggs* and she has voiced the fate of spring

Woman Holding a Balance

after Johannes Vermeer's 1664 painting of the same name

behind her:
a healing grace
the salvation of forgiveness
promise and sacrifice

before her:
value weighed
an equal measure
dignity and decorum

within her:
blood of generations
nurturing warmth
a round-cheeked future

Got Your Six

I burn my hand on the kettle
and you ask if I'm okay

yes, those sorts of wounds heal
to a shiny pink spot on my palm

sooner than we know it is gone
until someone reminds us

like when we met and I asked
the cause of the two long scars

on either side of your arm and
you told me of your rugby injury

how first you heard the crack
long before you felt the pain

but I barely notice those marks
now after these years except

when I fear you will hurt yourself
again especially when you're far

away and I'm not there to ask
if you're okay or see you shake it off.

Every Cell Expresses

ion channels   flowing through
neurons muscle cardiomyocytes oocytes
sometimes overexpressing
to be clamped off at the membrane
electrophysiology   voltage recorded
voltage applied   electrical access
to the inner workings   to how our
cells react to potassium and calcium
to be altered on the smallest level
in normal   and in diseased states

I've Been Loving You a Long Time

so long you have to look closely now to see:
how on a rainy night, I might rest my feet
on your thigh while we lounge on the couch
watching PBS murder mysteries;

how you still need me when you're looking for
something in the junk drawer even though it's
always right in front of your face because
we all need reminding of what's right there;

how the dog barks when we hug or kiss,
just as he's always done since he became ours
and how he likes to stand between us
every chance he gets, claiming me as his;

how the dog lies next to me on the couch,
paws against my thigh, my hand on his back

St. Ursula Makes an Appearance

While I load dog and child in the car
she speaks to me—I suppose because
lately I have been thinking of orders,
where they may take us this time or if
we'll stay here another estimated years—

She tells me, *Life is mostly legend anyway.*
Go where you are called and later when
you sit around a feast you will all tell stories
and the stories will vary from actual events,
but that doesn't matter in the end.

A Tale of Not-So-Ancient Mariners

How strange that evening—
the sea was like a carpet
held down by an island and
two smaller ships besides
ours, and you would think
us cursed, for our ship made
no progress, and try as she
might, the captain could
not steer her port nor
starboard, and so there we—
captain (girl), swashbuckler (I),
and appointed first-mate (dog)—
remained until the oven chimed,
and we jumped ship, howling
like the ghost pirates we
obviously became, treading
that rigid water all the way
to who we were before.

Gravitational

What Keeps Us Grounded

We can't just float away, you say,
and although it sometimes feels like
we might, I suppose you are right.

Walk like this, you say, taking big
strides. *This is how to walk on the moon*,
and I follow your example as best I can.

Did you know the Earth spins? you ask
while I stir pasta into boiling water,
and I say, *Yes* and *Be careful.*

Sometimes When I'm Walking

I am merely walking, but
sometimes each step
is a question mark and
itself the answer
       how
this body moves, slow
today, bending to press
my thumbprint in snow
to feel
       what
the earth must feel now,
not catatonic but asleep,
dreaming, turning still,
and this is
       why
I imagine the stars as
ships sailing a dark sea,
and know for a fact
I am myself
       who
with miles behind me
and more ahead, does not
want to regret I existed
half-full.

The Dog Days of Summer

everything moves more slowly now—
the air too thick for clouds to make their course
still as the dragonflies suspended above grass

a fly sits on the windowsill, and I let him
stay there held against his hungry will
just as I sit under a fan that holds me in place

I turn the pages in my book, the only thing
that dares make a sound this late morning

and the fan spins above me its ineffective task
but it cannot be blamed for its cheap one-speed
existence of a life lived out in a rental property

and even the dog cannot be moved by a squirrel
on the fence, and the squirrel spreads its body
to full length along the rail under the leafy oak

Dropped from the Clouds

to defy rationale
to willingly jump

free-fall 8,000 feet
less than a minute

instinct moves arms
in a breaststroke
(not what you want to do)

instinct moves feet
searching for a hold
(not what you want to do)

mind must be tricked
a meditation of sorts

before the second arrives
when the cord is pulled

Young Girl Reading

after Jean-Honoré Fragonard's 1770 painting of the same name

Jean-Honoré painted her innocent,
posture of a lady, book resting
in a gentle hand, eyes half-closed
(perhaps in study, perhaps in fantasy)

and how I would love to gaze over
her shoulder, read those blurred lines,
because that is the intrigue, allure
(perhaps in study, perhaps in fantasy)

Spaceship Pretend

faster and faster we figure-eight
around the couch and coffee table
super sonic speed you shout and
veer us off onto a tangent I thought
landed us in that open space
we don't use as a breakfast nook
but you say *this is not earth anymore*
we are on the moon and you show me
how to walk because I need to know
how to move my feet just right now
to stay semi-grounded in this half-
gravity state so I don't just float away
become an unidentified flying object
becoming more distant with each lightyear

Late Morning Walk

after Sylvia Plath's 1960 poem "Blackberrying"

Nobody, nothing, nothing but
the smoke of burning yard debris
carried on the autumn breeze,
nobody but me with my dog—
I talk to him, knowing he fully
understands, his terrier brain
far more advanced than mine,
and I guess at his responses,
answering for him the best
I possibly can. Then quiet
comes for a while and I think
how empty the streets are,
except for the bumble bees
who clumsily wobble around
my head on their search for
October blooms; they will find
them in our chrysanthemums.

My dog pulls at his leash with
each rustling of ferns, wild
rosemary, Carolina lupine,
but somehow, I cannot stop
thinking about blackberries.

LISA STICE

While Daddy's at Training,
Our Daughter Asks Questions

I don't know how to explain 35,000 feet—
all I can say is it's very high—yes, far above
our house and those trees, but no, not beyond
the moon or the stars—and *how far are those?*
but I don't know how to explain that either.

When will he be back?—so I count the days,
point to them on the calendar—*what is it like
in the sky?*—I say I know it's cold and difficult
to breathe, but I don't know how to explain
50 below or the partial pressure of oxygen.

She pretends to be an airplane—*can I skydive?*—
and I say when you are much older, but I don't
know if I'd want her to—she counts backwards
then jumps her couple inches—and my heart
rises before it falls back into place again.

Tea with Sun Tzu

I offer you this cup—
cast-iron vessel
decorated with a warrior

pattern, green matcha
steaming, my palm
warm and opened.

Teach me the tactics
to be serene and
indestructible, to be

resolved, to understand
the unfathomable
plans ahead of me.

Canis Major

Two creatures normally in perpetual motion
begin to retrograde, reach absolute zero,
dog with his nose up, daughter with finger

pointing at that Greater Dog who guards
us from his sky post, Sirius lighting
their faces, their expressions seemingly

saying *we are not terrestrial; we are stars*
evolved who fell to earth, photons, pulsars,
now in proper motion, now back at play

The School Project Asks, 'What Makes You a Star?'

To prove she is a good artist,
my daughter draws a spaceship
and her dog. *This is Seamus
about to board*, she explains.

I tell her about the stray Laika,
how she was one of the first
astronauts, but don't mention
Laika was never meant to return.

To prove she is a good artist,
my daughter draws a spaceship
with her dog inside. *This is Seamus
looking out at the stars*, she explains.

Happy Birthday, Joan Baez

high notes and scratchy static
from my record player
like *diamonds and rust*
like an old car that still starts
and rumbles down
dusty roads to a familiar
place   *here's to you*
a love song to a stranger
a memory of slower days
when I could sit under a tree—
maybe cherry or dogwood—
and read or do nothing at all
rooted as a *wildwood flower*
like you on the album cover
smiling and *forever young*

Faith

is a knowing that good wins out
in the end—even if the waiting
is long, a boy and a tree always
love each other, the wandering
vagabond winds his way home,
two birds discover they already
had what is best by story's end

is an expectation that truth holds
its ground—even if the crayon
loses its wrapping, it will still
color flowers red, even if a page
comes loose, we still remember
where it goes, even if someone
changes the story, we tell it right

LISA STICE

A Meditative Morning

kibble for the dog
and leftover pie for us
this is our breakfast

what is time, you ask
it is already passing
before my answer

who built me, you ask
I ask, *do you remember
being built*—you nod

Defensive

Dependants

after Randall Jarrell's 1969 poem "Eighth Air Force"

If, in the night we wake,
and think we hear thuds
outside the door
we hold our breaths
silence: is this fear?

The dog paces the hall between
our two rooms, his sniff and scratch
at bedside checks, circles, circles
until sleep invades: blink; blink; blink.
O sentry...this is your specialization:

This is war, too...but we don't ever say that,
like children who wake in morning; *big and little*,
as you like to say, *I'm Little-Big Girl*—
I will have to agree
marvel: this paradox!

We write to Daddy, send pictures, in emails—
our lives; this is how it's done.
Will they reach him?
I wash your hands and face after breakfast:
toss the crumbs away.

Somatic Growth

sometimes inconsistent with plotted charts—
    strategy   technical intelligence
theory   operational forces   art
of cells   proteins   hybrids bound to science
    in the making of bone and connective
muscles   non-linear   irregular
warfare inside the body—a collective
    battle book to explain a singular
symptom   blood gives microscopic answers
to neural doctrine and hormonal law
    to the principles of platelets   offer
available data   a caveat
of integrated chaos soon to be
    explained   on white paper

Petition

again, I say good-night,
sweet dreams, see you
in the morning, you need
your rest and so do I,
lie down, close your eyes,
you should be asleep,
should have been long ago,
it's late and getting later
as we speak, tomorrow
is almost here, again,
I say I don't want to hear
a sound until day, only
silence should be behind
this door, or at the most
quiet snoring, good-night

The Art of Being Snowed In

after Sun Tzu's book The Art of War

1. In all practicality, there will become a point when the snow loses its novelty. For the child, it is 10 minutes. For the dog, it is one day and one sleep. For the mother, it ends when the child loses interest.

2. The child breaks an icicle off the fence and wonders where it goes. Disappointment in the inability to bring her treasure indoors.

3. The dog plays like years have fallen from him. He tracks his own tracks.

4. Those rules are for the first day.

5. Pull the shutters closed to keep the cold out, but sun also remains outside. Such are the gains and losses of cabin fever.

6. Assemble a puzzle, then another, then another. Begin again.

7. The dog will sleep more than his usual.

8. Each day walk a different path through the yard, for the one you walked before will be icy and treacherous. Check the mail in hopes it will arrive this day.

9. Great sympathy for the dog who treads lightly on a refrozen surface. Still, one hind leg falls through now and then.

10. Stretch your resources. Paint more slowly. Ration food supplies. Dance, play accordion, and make up songs in between other diversions.

Bad News Is Often Revealed in the Kitchen

Perhaps, I washed fruit—
an apple, some grapes,
it really doesn't matter—
most likely because I was
hungry or bored or
just in a habit and isn't it
so easy to forget the details
—whether we fold
the towels to the left or
the right, whether the dog
woke at 4 a.m. or 5:30 a.m.,
whether I swept the kitchen
floor that day—as if my shadow
moved without me, following
automatic synapses while
I was really somewhere else
entirely.

Night Café

after Vincent van Gogh's 1888 painting of the same name

silent as night should be

heads bowed
some resting
on folded arms

I am on the other side
of the room
alone in a corner

Perennials

On this overcast day, my husband plants
candytufts because they last, will come back
even when you think they've gone, sweet
scent returning year after year. He wants
them in the ground before the rain, light
drizzle wetting his hair and shirt as he digs,
hunched over with his spade, and the dog
half-sleeps nearby on a long leash tethered
to the magnolia that leans a bit since the last
big storm. He wants them in the ground before
he leaves again, for a shorter time than last.

Seamus Heaney's To-Do List

dig with bare hands

see the earth
under fingernails

listen to the cows
chew their cud

fall in love then
fall in love again
with a city

bring a brother back
with pen and ink

rebuild streets
with words in rows

go far far away

speak from behind
a podium

hands balancing
amnesty

find the miracles
in the now-and-then
in the often-missed

stand on the foothill
and shout

walk on air
against your better judgment

Measures

and means—quantifications
in the action phase: time between
arrival and what will come later

laid out chronologically and refined
to a standard—addressed then
redressed to fit the form already made

there then here in civil augmentation
in contracted support in combatant
logistics—dispatched to frays, edgings

Explaining the Summer Solstice to a Nearly Four-Year-Old

It is night, I say
but the bedazzling
brightness radiates
from around curtains
and she doesn't believe
me as I try to explain
the turn of the earth
and our distance
from the sun, but
I am proud, in a way,
of how luminous
she looks in her
defiance to sleep,
how she stands
arms folded holding
onto an incandescent
belief that the world
spins on logic
and that everything
was will always be.

Another Training

Fog has traveled far to rest on windows,
to condense itself on pine needles and
fall with the sound of light rain, to fool us
this morning when we step on the wet lawn,
to make my dog hesitate before he
steps from cement to grass, first high-stepping
then running as the weary, fallen fog
transforms my dog into a wild, wet beast.

Now, he tracks, zigzagging the ground, turning
back on himself again and again like
he is searching for someone lost, perhaps,
maybe you whom he expected home soon
with your scent now washing away, fading.
The dog is a dog again, howling.

The Other David

after Donatello's circa-1440s bronze sculpture of David

This is the one who looks less equal
to a giant, one who would surprise
an entire village and later be written
about, dictated by the voice of God.

This is the one who is dark and slight,
his helmet decorated with laurels, left
hand on hip, right hand grasping the hilt
of a sword wider than his arm, legs casual.

This is the one I would root for, uncommon
hero, and see how even Goliath admires him,
how the wing of that giant's helmet caresses
David's leg, how the beard hugs David's foot.

LISA STICE

Lying to Our Daughter

Our daughter asks why
we are putting her stuffed animals
in bags, why we're unplugging
lamps, TV, phones, router, etc.,
why we're rearranging furniture,
why we're moving little things
to top shelves in closets.

We say *we're just picking up
a bit before we leave* because
we don't want to tell her a hurricane
is coming. It's like how we tell her
*you can grow up to be whatever
you want* because we hope when
she arrives there, it might be true.

Our daughter asks where we are going.
We say *we're going to visit Uncle
Paddy* because we want to make this
evacuation feel like a vacation. It's like
how we never want her to be afraid
even though we know a hurricane
is really just a little storm among many.

Rock Collection

mostly gravel:
aggregate
a conglomerate
of minerals combined
polymictal, oligomictal
compacted and concreted

one piece of quartz:
silicon and
oxygen tetrahedra
continuous framework
semi-precious
the one she calls a diamond

Frictional

Standard Equation

Resistance is the coefficient
of two surfaces multiplied
by the normal force upon them—

static, sliding, rolling fluid

movements converted
into energy, consequences

subscripts making traction
independent of velocity.

LISA STICE

Warning

If you say when she is an infant
I can take her anywhere
She hardly ever cries, so easy

those brags will rise and rise
until she floods you with whines
and tantrums in grocery aisles

partly cloudy moods followed by
torrents of tears and screams
and just when temps have reached

their highest and you feel like
you must find shelter anywhere
her index falls and she looks at you

and it's clear that she loves you
and that you love this stormy girl
with all her highs and lows.

Plans Always Change

and I should know this by now,
that I should never expect anything,
get too excited, begin imagining
the door opening, having to quiet
that dog's welcoming bark lest
he wake my daughter from her
midnight sleep, begin imagining
my daughter's disbelief when she
sees Daddy frying eggs at the stove
in the morning, of course, it's my
fault, all this disappointment, of
course I'd get the text at 1:30something
in the a.m. that another training
day's been added and flights home
need to be rearranged, and of course,
I can't help but worry that a seat
won't be found at such short notice,
more *I'll let you know when I know
something,* always the unknown

Daughter (5), Mother (39)

She is a magpie, and I am a blue jay—
or perhaps she would say it's the other way round.

Either way, we are always tittering or squawking,
or going on and on with the *did-you-know.*

But we are birds of a feather, as the saying goes,
her intonations mimicking mine—*no way.*

She says, *I look like you, only better*—yes,
that one is smart and tricky and knows far more

than anyone might expect. I notice sometimes
I mimic her—a unique turn of phrase like

we are the same only different. And it's true
because we know oh so well who we are.

Downpour

During the rain, we couldn't see
the new house across the street
or the street itself, the loblolly
pines in our backyard or azalea
that grow along our outer wall—

Looking out, we couldn't see
much of anything except rain
smeared and beaten, desperately
clinging to the windows, and
we heard it too and tried to calm
the dog while I held him tightly
and you said *don't be scared
it's only raining raindrops*—

Then after the rain, it all looked
different with the dog panting
more slowly while what remained
of the downpour dripped off eaves
or settled sleepily into the low areas,
so we opened the door and walked
out to scattered purple blossoms,
birds visiting the feeder and butterflies
tasting the flowers still on bushes,
green anoles crawling along the fence,
and you disrupting the puddles.

The Key

after the 1946 series of paintings by Jackson Pollock

preformed figures
    semblance of
shape   of
people   sitting
    of a man   bent
in prayer   of a woman
    bent eating   her
plate full   perhaps
      an infant
    in a cradle   perhaps
a dog curled   in his bed
    perhaps a visitor
    at the door
      perhaps
a fire lit   coals
    hot   hills
distant   turn the key
    in the lock
    before you   leave

Headstrong

I'm sorry catches in the throat
and bruises in that wavering
hesitation like a rock falling
back to earth. See how it curves
under the skin, twists and cuts
as it hugs the voice box.

I forgive sways like a tamarack—
hackmatack, red larch, juniper,
larix laricina—of the low-lands
with roots in cool mud and branches
in the soft air where we hold
the belief we are stronger than wind.

The end is as blue as slag and twice
as worthless. This is where I say
I never meant it, and this is where
you say it doesn't matter anymore
because words are less than
clouds and leaves and stone.

Saoirse Is
for my Saoirse

hair falling in eyes
scrapes on knees

red paint across a page
sparkles on the floor

holding my hands
to walk up my legs

towers made of books
then the books read

chasing the dog and
being chased by the dog

questions and questions
songs out of key

blankets and pillows
quiet in sleep

For a Moment

found on page 608 of American Triptych by Pearl S. Buck

step slowly   back
again   a world
subterranean hours

the last page   silently
finished   doubt gambled
as solid as delight   a book

varieties of history
use   a book   that last
page   a heap of ashes

a voice   stilled in sleep
exhausted with awareness
closed eyes   spared nothing

to know such love
to be afraid   this power
flooding fumbled pages

This One Is Mine

after William J. Rupertus' "The Rifleman's Creed"

There she is. The small one over
there with the awkward run that
every five-year-old has, but look
there how her backpack reaches
there to her knees, how she balances
there on one leg then quickly moves
there to pick up litter out of rocks while
I wait here in the car line and watch.
There are others like her (maybe), but
this one is mine. I am useless, it is
true, without her. She and I know
there was no time before her. And
she has a father. We teach her to
be clean and ready. And she has a
brother (who is a terrier). We are
there to teach how weaknesses can
be strengths, how small ones can be
there right next to everyone, or even
there somewhere ahead. We are a part
of each other. From here, I watch her
there. Look how she pulls everything
into her sights, ready to move from
there, clean into wherever she wants.

Accordion Practice

My daughter plays *Rock-a-Bye Baby*,
sings along sweet and slow, each note
deliberate, each word a small flickering
flame. Then I say *play whatever you like*
and she presses the air button, the pull
of the bellows like the scrape of a match.
Her raised eyebrow, a warning: the fuze
will be lit, and the accordion will explode
with the chaos of her own creation.

Internet News

notice
a tipping point
technology
files
convenience
available whenever
listen
it's gone
just like
a knack for
endless focus
interest
should be heard
consumed
they're doing other things
produced content
audience of the listeners

And We Know Her Daddy Didn't Teach Her
to Shoot Like That

These are the words of the father
of the two-year-old whose birthday
we attend this chilly, windy afternoon.

He is correct although I think he meant
his statement as a jab, made to mock
my husband in front of his Marines.

I am proud, though, proud this is the first
time my daughter has even touched a toy gun
(blue and white plastic with suction cup darts),

proud that my husband is not embarrassed
by all these laughing men who call him
"the liberal" and blame me for the way he is,

proud that my daughter sent that dart through
the smallest circle of tissue paper and shared
her prize (a Twix) with a pregnant guest.

Don't Hesitate

When skipping down a grocery aisle,
each step constructing an acoustic circuit,
maneuvers, stratagems combat boredom.

How adorable a woman says, but her tone
says *you've lost authority over this one.*

Another woman says it flat out *manage your
child*, but how can a child manage to be a child
when sabotaged every skip of the way.

Tensile

Breaking Point

There is always a maximum.
I think I have reached it,
but from the fissure in my side
blood does not pour, instead
ink and graphite seep. Give me
paper to soak it all up, give me
others' poems to fill the empty.

LISA STICE

Yesterday Is Extinct

bones risen from clay
melted like crayons
left on the sidewalk

or ice cream on hands
not in the process of
melting but already

lost to some past we've
set aside with the wicker
rocking horse I rode

when I was a child and
my daughter has outgrown
her own bones rising

stretching and ready to run
like a flightless bird
wild into darkness

Homecomings

are often quiet, 2:30 a.m. sort of events—
deadbolt slides, door opens slowly,
dog and I wake to *hello*, rucksack and
suitcase placed by the door, dog jumps
for licks, hugs and kisses, I'm so glad
you're back, *I'm so glad to be back*,
then it's off to sleep as if this is any night

Man with Unhealthy Complexion
Listening to the Sound of the Sea
after Salvador Dalí's 1929 painting of the same name

he is seated in a chair
in his living room
with the blinds drawn

raises an opalescent hand
cups it to his ear
and believes it's a shell

    when he was a boy
    he walked the beaches
    built castles to topple

    his skin was dark
    warm to the touch
    from his coming and going

but now he listens
to the dust settling
believes he is the sea

his body a curled wave
his innards kelp
his breath an ebb and flow

My Daughter Wants to Be a Surfer

she is only four now, years
from when she'll be old enough
and strong enough to stand on
a board and ride a wave, now
she thinks it will be stable like
a butte or mesa, her arms out for
the look, for feeling the freedom

I tell her *hang ten* as she bends
her knees, her arms like wings,
her face straight ahead, here
in the hallway on the hardwood,
and I show her with my hand
the symbol for what I said, my
thumb and pinky at antipodes,
a narrow channel in the middle

Autumn Change

No more pinching off the mum buds. We'll let them bloom,
look like a ball of fire. Bees will dig their holes and sleep
until our terrier digs them up to drop the slumbering gift
at our feet, but I digress. My daughter's growth-curve curves
down, a dormant sort of growing that keeps her smaller than
her friend's two-year-old sister, that surprises strangers when
she says, *look that's an octagon*, not a full stop, just enough
to wonder, but I digress. I noticed the days shortening, fog
wandering in with morning's coolness. Soon we will camp
in the backyard, unroll the tent and sleeping bags, find where
we stored the lantern, and we will wake, feeling younger.

Cecilia and the Weasel

after Leonardo da Vinci's circa-1491 painting "Lady with an Ermine"

There you are, over my shoulder,
in the shadows. I am oil on wood,
fluid and solid—real as blood
and bone. Forget me not and keep
me in the light. Find me on the hunt.

Discussion of Death Over Dessert

Ghosts live inside us, she says,
*we call them spirits, and they
are what make our shadows.*

We are eating yogurt—the kind
we have to flip and mix—not
healthy at all, but with chocolate.

Sometimes I've heard her talk
to the spirit inside her, sometimes
to free-floating forms or wisps.

I like this yogurt, she says, *I like
chocolate.* She doesn't mix much,
eats until the morsels are gone.

She explains, *Wisps tell me stories,
scary stories. I want to make them
into a movie that's even better.*

My daughter has stopped at the sweetness,
but I keep eating, scrape the soured milk
with my spoon and bring it to my mouth.

Here We Are

in the wait
again

this limbo of
here for now

then where
we guess

75% chance
of staying

25% chance
of the west

10% chance
of headquarters

5% chance
of overseas

and the rest
go to anywhere

Cleft Speech

wind at play

    in autumn   leaves

      gray   squirrel   leaping

   cricket in the warmth   of twilight

green tree frogs' chatter   on repeat

   shuffle of feet   in winter grass

   the dog's   nervous yip

   blackbirds on the lawn

old vinyl   on the   portable player

   listen   lean in

       be patient

Good-night

The moon arcs across the sky
like a stone passed hand to hand
to hand, disappearing behind
a fist of trees, only seemingly
gone when night rolls over
to morning.
    And while it was
still night, my daughter woke
three separate times, saying
she couldn't sleep. I showed
her proof of the darkness
outside.
    Now the sun peeks
between loblolly pines, and
the girl slumbers in her room,
the house seemingly empty,
me, with only my journal and
this curled-up dog.

Observance

The Lenten roses are in bloom again
(as they always are this time of year)
night coaster, royal heritage, pink
frost, dashing groomsmen, romantic
getaway, honeymoon French kiss.

And we have given you up again
(as we always do this time of year)
finning, self-contained breathing,
parachutes, mock cities, survive,
evade, resist, escape, night maneuvers.

Blue

after Pablo Picasso's 1902 painting "Blue Nude"

she almost disappears completely
into the (sadness, depression,
isolation) what we like to simply
call blue until we have frozen her

solidly curled up in protection
her body a swirl an exhale
of carbon dioxide crystalized
then vaporized then gone

Today, I Am

words moved from paper
to hard drive—originally
in pen—it is not a cursive
kind of morning with this
Southern heat—I am sloppy
print still in pajamas and
my hair unbrushed, no
breakfast in my stomach—
no need for loops and swirls

Magnetic

Old Faithful

lies at my feet right now
as I write these words

his body stretched out
front paws under chin

hind legs pulled in
ears pointed and listening

later, he will follow me
as I move from room to room

just as he followed me from
east coast to west coast then

west coast to east coast
just as he will again

LISA STICE

Seamus and I Meet the Ghosts of Carlo and Emily Dickinson

after the circa-1862 poem "I started Early – Took my Dog"
by Emily Dickinson

On an early walk – tired –
we stopped a bit to take
a rest – Seamus sniffed
dandelion greens and grass –

I admired a robin skipping
on a neighbor's lawn – then
something made us turn
our heads – look down

the street – a woman all
in white with a great brown
dog – not walking really –
more like floating – Seamus

and I knew them straight
away – Emily and Carlo –
the street became a sandy
shore – the wind became

the ocean's roar – little
dog barked a happy greeting –
good-morning, I wished
the two – they halted

there before us – Emily
bent to pet my tiny dog –

Such a lovely nubby tail
he has – Seamus wagged

his nub in gratefulness –
and just as strangely as
they came – they left us –
standing on a street again.

As We Look at Real Estate Sites

one of these days you say
I sigh and say yes although
that house with a garden

seems so far away from
potted plants scattered around
this rented yard *one of these days*

you say we will load terracotta
rooted flowers and herbs
onto a moving van one last time

and *one of these days* you say
we'll let all those plants stretch
their roots in stagnant ground

How to Play Like a Four-Year-Old

be loud when you screech like a bat of darkness
and remember some animals can talk – pretend dogs,
animals who wear clothes, unusually colored horses –
but some animals can talk only in their own language –
real dogs, non-magical cats, bats of darkness (of course)

dance slightly off from the beat of the music, then
spin and spin and spin (an actual four-year-old
will always outdo you), then run as fast as you can
through kitchen and dining room, run much like
a cheetah, stopping to take deep breaths (your breaths will be real)

make up rules that change as the game takes you
and remember that games are anything that can be
played – dress up, don't step on the short pieces
of hardwood, chase the dog – most of the time a tie
will be declared and all will celebrate (likely more dance)

LISA STICE

This Morning

with the weather unusually warm
I walked barefoot into the garden
to goad the vegetables into growing
to entice the flowers into opening

and there I found a radish, tumid,
large as a plum or a stone to toss,
ready to be snipped, ready to crunch,
its peppery burn tickling my throat

Rare and Used

time smells like dust
cracked spines and
faded gold inlay
yellow pages darkening
still to a soft brown
comfortable like
the afghan my great-aunt
knitted for my parents'
wedding gift or
the quilt a great-
great-aunt stitched
from resurrected men's
suits and I can see
the face of my grandmother's
grandfather just as clearly
as I feel I know Felix
who dedicated this book
of Keats poems to Rose

Can You Hear It

listen carefully to this joy
listen as it begins a quiet breathing
listen to the inhale then exhale
listen how it changes to a cough
listen for the clearing of the voice
listen for the announcement
listen carefully to what I have to say:
listen to your breathing
listen how your breath comes in a quiet brook
listen how your breath exits a cascade
listen to how your voice sounds
listen to what you have to say

Good Customer

I wish I could remember faces with their names
and, likewise, be remembered for my order
like in black-and-white movies in which someone
always has *a usual*. I wish each day were usual
with the simplicity of deciding what to eat, whether
apple pie or cherry, a la mode or not. I suppose
by *usual*, I mean *ordinary*, *simple*. I wish each hour
could be a gradient of gray, easy on the eyes and
certainly easy on the stomach. Nostalgia looks like
a ghost, no face and names that are hard to place.
I'd like to call it *Innocent*, but it isn't that, and isn't
Better either. It's all just sort of grainy-like, like
a photograph I tried to take while sitting at a table.

LISA STICE

Reading Szymborska During a Snow Storm

I turn another page—this one dog-eared
from some other time. Bergamot steeps
in my cup as snow grows deeper outside.

For a long while, the only sounds: paper
sliding along paper and a faucet's
light stream from down the hall, then

a word sets fire to a thought and I reach
for my pen—the dog rings his bell, but still
I attempt to write. He is unyielding.

And after he's left prints circling the yard,
after he's done his business, I rub his feet
warm and kiss the top of his head because

I love him, and that moment when idea
would explode into poem has passed, but
I don't despair—more will burn again.

Funny Girl

She told me once that a dog
with a cat on his back could
climb a tree, but I don't
remember the punchline,
and now she tells knock-knock
jokes that end before the
blah, blah, blah who's there,
and still, somehow, they're
funny and make me laugh
the sort of laugh that exercises
my core in such a way that
the next morning, I feel
the tightness to remind me
just how deep those chuckles
were, so I say tell me another.

Norwich Terrier Explains How to Dig a Hole

begin with purpose
an end-goal to unearth
a secret: a bumble bee
sleeping underground
or a squirrel's hoard
or a root that winds
its way and begs you
to keep tossing dirt
until a small hill grows
behind you, then lie down
and rest in the coolness
of your creation

3 Haiku

all is gray this day—
leafless maple, sky before
snow, tea in my cup

❖ ❖ ❖

this dappled night sky
broth simmered for millennia—
I drink it tonight

❖ ❖ ❖

small girl with small dog
she says, *he makes me braver*
milkweed seed with breeze

Where Have You Gone, Joe DiMaggio?

up in the attic, collecting dust
with the wicker rocking horse
with the view finder
    click: Pyramids of Giza without crowds
    click: Parthenon without graffiti
    click: Niagara Falls without kitsch

in the garage, dry and cracked
with the little-league catcher's mitt
with the baby toys all boxed up
    lamb mobile
    jungle friends bouncer
    rattles and teething rings

in the street, empty and quiet
with the dead leaves' susurrations
with the old dog sleeping on the porch
    no noisy basketballs bouncing
    no bicycle tires skidding
    no crack of ball and bat colliding

Our Lady of the Wayside

yes, let's take our time
stop and stretch our legs
take in the landscape
appreciate the edges
foothills and mesas and
sagebrush drying brown

we have St. Christopher
in the glovebox with maps
we no longer use with folded
papers and my old straw hat
crumpled on top of insurance
and registration and manual

whisper to us St. Drogo
lead us to St. Peter Chanel
to the coast and the sea
rise and fall on the waves
with saints Brendan and
Nicholas catch fire with
St. Elmo for the rest of life.

ACKNOWLEDGEMENTS

I am grateful to the editors of the following literary magazines, in which some of these poems first appeared—some in slightly different versions. Additionally, some poems also appeared during my participation in the January 2018 Tupelo Press 30/30 Project:

"**Accordion Practice**" first appeared in *3Elements Review* No. 18, spring 2018

"**The Art of Being Snowed In**" first appeared in *The Bangor Literary Journal* No. 6, winter 2018

"**Blue**" first appeared in *The Ekphrastic Review* Nov. 30, 2017

"**Canis Major**" first appeared in *Inklette* No. 6, spring 2018

"**Cecilia and the Weasel**" first appeared in *Anti-Heroin Chic,* Aug. 4, 2017

"**Counting the Casualties**" first appeared in *As You Were: The Military Review* Vol. 8, spring/summer 2018

"**Dependants**" first appeared in *1932 Quarterly,* summer 2017

"**The Dog Days of Summer**" first appeared in *The Wild Word* No. 19: "The Long Days of Summer," summer 2017

"**Downpour**" first appeared in *Moledro Magazine* No. 6, June 2017

"**Explaining the Summer Solstice to a Nearly Four-Year-Old**" first appeared in the *Peeking Cat Anthology 2017,* Peeking Cat Literary 2017

"**Got Your Six**" first appeared in the anthology *Proud to Be: Writing by American Warriors, Vol. 8,* Southeast Missouri State University Press, 2019

"**Happy Birthday, Joan Baez**" first appeared in *The Song Is...* literary blog, September 2017

"**Headstrong**" first appeared in *The Wrath-Bearing Tree* January 2018

"**How to Play Like a Four-Year-Old**" first appeared in *Dodging the Rain*, October 2018

"**I've Been Loving You a Long Time**" was shortlisted for The Bangor Poetry Competition 2018 (hosted by *The Bangor Literary Journal*)

"**Late Morning Walk**" first appeared in *Dodging the Rain*, October 2018

"**Man with Unhealthy Complexion Listening to the Sound of the Sea**" first appeared in *The Woven Tale Press* Vol. 5, No. 3 in spring 2017

"**Measures**" first appeared in the anthology *Proud to Be: Writing by American Warriors, Vol. 8,* Southeast Missouri State University Press, 2019

"**A Meditative Morning**" first appeared in the literary journal *Interstice*, May 2018

"**My Daughter Wants to Be a Surfer**" first appeared in the literary journal *Interstice*, May 2018

"**Night Café**" first appeared in the Vincent Van Gogh-inspired anthology *Resurrection of a Sunflower,* Pski's Porch Publishing 2017

"**Norwich Terrier Explains How to Dig a Hole**" first appeared in *Happy2 Pure Slush* Vol. 15, spring 2018

"**Observance**" first appeared in *Picaroon* No. 1, March 2019

"**Ode to the Rotary Phone**" first appeared in *Chantwood Magazine* No. 10, September 2017

"**Rare and Used**" first appeared in *Moledro Magazine* No. 6, June 2017

"**Ritual Hunts**" first appeared in *Gravel*, November 2017

"**Rock Collection**" first appeared in *Skylight 47* issue No. 11, autumn 2018

"**The School Project Asks, 'What Makes You a Star?'**" first appeared in *Bold + Italic* No. 5, January 2020

"**Seamus Heaney's To-Do List**" first appeared in *Sheila-Na-Gig* Vol. 2.3, spring 2018

"**Somatic Growth**" first appeared in *8 Poems Journal* issue No. 1.3, September 2018

"**Sometimes When I'm Walking**" first appeared in *So It Goes: The Literary Journal of the Kurt Vonnegut Museum and Library, Vol. 7,* fall 2018. That year's theme was "A little more common decency."

"**Spaceship Pretend**" first appeared in *Minetta Review* fall 2017

"Tea with Sun Tzu" first appeared in *Sierra Nevada Review* Vol. 29, May 2018

"This Morning" first appeared in *Escapism Literary Magazine* No. 2, summer 2017

"3 haiku" first appeared in *Bonsai: a journal of haiku & other small poems* (a project of *The 13 Alphabet Magazine*), May 2018

"This One Is Mine" first appeared in *Pure Slush: 7 Deadly Sins* Vol. 7 "Pride," spring 2019

"Today, I Am" first appeared in *The Song Is ...* literary blog, July 2018

"Yesterday Is Extinct" first appeared in *Artemis Journal* Vol. 25, May 2018

"Where Have You Gone, Joe DiMaggio?" first appeared in *The Ocotillo Review* (Kallisto Gaia Press) Vol. 2.2, summer 2018

"While Daddy's at Training, Our Daughter Asks Questions" first appeared in *The Honest Ulsterman*, June 2018

"Woman Holding a Balance" first appeared in *Dodging the Rain*, October 2018

NOTES

In my first poetry collection, *Uniform* (Aldrich Press, 2016), I experimented with the poetry of erasure—cutting poems out of the military briefings, speeches, and literature I encountered while navigating my found realities as a woman married to a United States Marine. Erasure of these texts provided me with a sense of control at times when I most felt my life controlled by the Corps, and it helped me to carve my place within tradition.

In *Permanent Change of Station* (Middle West Press, 2018), I focused on a different technique, that of borrowed language and phrases from children's literature and Sun Tzu's *The Art of War*.

In *Forces*, I pull inspiration from military jargon, literature, and art. When various aspects of life pull me in different directions, spin me around, or attempt to stop me altogether, finding a way to bring calm and beauty to the chaos gives me strength.

To ensure full disclosure and translation, in addition to explaining some of the military jargon, I give credit here to the words, events, and art that inspired my own:

Operational

"Counting the Casualties": On July 10, 2017, a U.S. Marine Corps KC-130T "Hercules" cargo plane crashed in Leflore County, Mississippi, killing all 16 people on board.

"Devising the Strategy": The title and first line are borrowed from *The Utility of Force: The Art of War in the Modern World* by retired British Gen. Rupert Smith; the last three words borrowed from the title.

"I've Been Loving You a Long Time": The title is borrowed from a lyric in "A Rainy Night in Soho," written by Shane McGowan and performed by The Pogues, a Celtic punk band that started in the 1980s.

"St. Ursula Makes an Appearance": St. Ursula is the patron saint of education, teachers, and students. The italicized words are my imagining of what she how she would instruct me.

"A Tale of Not So Ancient Mariners": This poem is inspired by "The Rime of the Ancient Mariner" by English Romantic poet Samuel Taylor Coleridge (1772-1834).

Gravitational

"Dropped from the Clouds": The title is borrowed from the title of first section of *The Mysterious Island* by French novelist, poet, and playwright Jules Verne (1828-1905).

"Happy Birthday, Joan Baez": Italicized words are song titles. Joan Baez (born Jan. 9, 1941) is a contemporary folk artist and counterculture icon.

Defensive

"The Art of Being Snowed In": This poem is inspired by the structure and style of Sun Tzu's *The Art of War*. Sun Tzu was a military leader and strategist in ancient China, circa 500 B.C.E.

"Seamus Heaney's To-Do List": Italicized lines are from Seamus Heaney's poem "The Gravel Walks" and his gravestone. Seamus Heaney (1939-2013) was an Irish poet and playwright, and was awarded the 1995 Nobel Prize in Literature.

Frictional

"Standard Equation": This poem is inspired by the standard equation for friction, $\mu = F/N$

"For a Moment": This poem utilizes erasure of page 608 of *American Triptych* by American novelist Pearl S. Buck (1892-1973). Buck won the Pulitzer Prize in 1938 for *The Good Earth*, and was awarded the 1938 Novel Prize in Literature.

"This One Is Mine": Written by U.S. Marine Maj. Gen. William H. Rupertus (1889-1945), then the commander of the San Diego Marine Barracks. Written in the days following Japan's attack on Pearl Harbor, Dec. 7, 1941, "The Rifleman's Creed" is intended to instill a common sense of purpose and responsibility while establishing a bond between the professional and his/her tool. The creed, once taught by drill instructors at Marine basic training, is still often referenced in military and pop culture.

Tensile

"Breaking Point": This poem is inspired by the physics of tension.

"Blue": The curled up posture of the woman in Pablo Picasso's *Blue Nude* (1902) reminds me of the hurts we sometimes carry far too long. The Spanish painter, sculptor, printmaker, and ceramist lived 1881-1973.

Magnetic

"Reading Szymborska During a Snow Storm": This poem is variously inspired by the life and work of Polish poet Wislawa Szymborska (1923-2012). She was awarded the 1996 Nobel Prize in Literature.

"Where Have You Gone, Joe DiMaggio?": The title is borrowed from a line in "Mrs. Robinson" (1968), a song by the 1960s folk-rock duo Paul Simon and Art Garfunkel. A Major League Baseball player, Joe DiMaggio (1914-1999) played center field for the New York Yankees.

"Our Lady of the Wayside": Madonna Della Strada (In English, "Our Lady of the Wayside" or "Saint Mary of the Good Road") was said to have protected Spanish Basque Ignatius of Loyola (1491-1556) during battle in his service as a young soldier. He would later become a priest and theologian, and co-founder of the Catholic religious order called the Society of Jesus (the "Jesuits").

THANKS

Thanks to my little muses, Saoirse and Seamus, for the endless inspirations they provide.

Thanks to my husband for his support and help with editing.

Thanks to my parents, Lois and Robert Houlihan, and my brother Patrick Houlihan for their encouragement even from great distances away. Thanks for giving me the love of reading and words.

Thanks to my writing and literature professors at Mesa State College (now Colorado Mesa University) and University of Alaska Anchorage for all that you taught me and for keeping in touch all these years after graduation.

Thanks to my fellow poets, fiction writers, and non-fiction writers who, through the low-residency Master of Fine Arts program at the University of Alaska Anchorage, became fast friends who continue to be a wonderful support network.

Thanks to the many writers I've met at past conferences and on-line.

Thanks especially to fellow writers Eric Chandler (*Kekekabic* and *Hugging This Rock*); Colin D. Halloran (*American Etiquette, Icarian Flux,* and *Shortly Thereafter*); Andria Williams (*The Longest Night: A Novel*); and Randy Brown (*So Frag & So Bold* and *Welcome to FOB Haiku*). I have enjoyed sharing our mutual war stories of parenthood, poetry, and military life, and look forward to many more years of such adventures.

Thanks to *Inklette Magazine* for giving me the opportunity, as a poetry editor, to help other poets share their words with the world.

Thanks to *Military Spouse Book Review*, *Military Spouse Fine Artists Network*, and *Veterans Writing Project* for giving me the opportunity to contribute to military writers and artists communities.

Thanks to the poets, writers, and artists who inspired some of these poems.

Thanks to the literary journals that gave some of these poems homes.

Thanks to Middle West Press for letting these poems live as a family in this collection.

Thanks to all those who read poetry.

Thanks to all those who read to children.

ABOUT THE WRITER

Lisa Stice is the author of the previously published poetry collections Uniform (Aldrich Press, 2016) and *Permanent Change of Station* (Middle West Press, 2018), and the poetry chapbook *Desert* (Prolific Press, 2018). Her work appears widely in literary journals and anthologies worldwide, the latter including *Beyond the Hill* (Lost Tower Publications, 2017); and *Nuclear Impact: Broken Atoms in Our Hands* (Shabda Press, 2017).

Stice's poem "Pursuit" was the 2020 military-family category poetry winner in the Col. Darron L. Wright Memorial Writing Awards, administered annually by the literary journal *Line of Advance*.

In 2017, her poem "Dear Wadih Sa'adeh" was selected as an honorable mention in the poetry category in that year's volume of the *Proud to Be: Writing by American Warriors* anthology series, published by Southeast Missouri State University Press. Her poem "A Quick Lunch from the Noodle Stand" was nominated for a 2016 Pushcart Prize by *The Magnolia Review*.

Stice is a poetry editor for *Inklette Magazine,* and often serves as an editor and mentor with various other writing organizations. The poet holds a Bachelor of Arts in English literature from Mesa State College (now Colorado Mesa University), Grand Junction, Colo., and a Master of Fine Arts in Creative Writing and Literary Arts from the University of Alaska, Anchorage.

She currently lives in North Carolina with her husband, daughter, and a beloved Norwich Terrier named Seamus.

You can learn more about her on-line at: lisastice.wordpress.com

Or follow her on Facebook and Twitter: @LisaSticePoet

ABOUT THE COVER

Upper image, front cover:

The oil-on-canvas "Lady Holding a Balance" was painted around the year 1664 by the Dutch Baroque painter Johannes Vermeer (1632-1674). The artist is noted today for his extravagant use of expensive blue, orange and gold pigments, and for his seemingly photorealistic depictions of light.

Vermeer produced fewer than 50 paintings during his lifetime. Usually, he painted portraits. In modern popular culture, he is perhaps most recognized for his "Girl With Pearl Earring" (1665), which inspired a 1999 historical novel and a 2003 movie. Thirty-four of Vermeer's paintings are still in existence; "Lady Holding a Balance" is now in the Widener Collection of the U.S. National Gallery of Art.

The painting, sometimes also known as "Goldweigher" or "Girl Weighing Pearls," is allegorical, in that it juxtaposes a woman who is judging the worth of material items, with a background painting that depicts a Christian story of the Last Judgment. Further complicating possible interpretations, the woman may be pregnant. Perhaps she is a secularized representation of Mary, mother of Jesus?

National Gallery curator Arthur K. Wheelock Jr. writes of the painting:

> This scene has religious implications that seem related to Saint Ignatius of Loyola's instructions, in his Spiritual Exercises, that the faithful, prior to meditating, first examine their conscience and weigh their sins as if facing Judgment Day. Only such introspection could lead to virtuous choices along the path of life. "Woman Holding a Balance" thus allegorically urges us to conduct our lives with temperance and moderation. [...]

For more information, visit:
www.nga.gov/collection/art-object-page.1236

Lower image, front cover:

Apr. 16, 2011—A Marine with 3rd Marine Special Operations Battalion, U.S. Marine Corps Forces, Special Operations Command, conducts a High-Altitude, High-Opening ("HAHO") jump as part of a Double-Bag Static-Line parachute course in Wendover, Utah. The course was taught by personnel from the 2nd Marine Special Operations Battalion paraloft and the Airborne Mobile Training Team, and was designed to give Marines a basic understanding of HAHO operations. *Photo by Lance Cpl. Kyle McNally.*

Disclaimer: "The appearance of U.S. Department of Defense (DOD) visual information does not imply or constitute DOD endorsement."

Author photo (back cover) by Andria Williams

DID YOU ENJOY THIS BOOK?

Tell your friends and family about it, or post your thoughts via social media sites, like Facebook and Twitter! On-line communities that serve military families, veterans, and service members are also ideal places to help spread the word about this book, and others like it!

You can also share a quick review on websites for other readers, such as Goodreads.com. Or offer a few of your impressions on bookseller websites, such as Amazon.com and BarnesandNoble.com!

Better yet, recommend the title to your favorite local librarian, poetry society or book club leader, museum gift store manager, or independent bookseller! There is nothing more powerful in business of publishing than a shared review or recommendation from a friend.

We appreciate your support! We'll continue to look for new stories and voices to share with our readers. Keep in touch!

You can write us at:

Middle West Press LLC
P.O. Box 1153
Johnston, Iowa 50131-9420

Or visit: www.middlewestpress.com

❖　❖　❖

Other poetry collections from Middle West Press LLC:

Welcome to FOB Haiku:
War Poetry from Inside the Wire,
by Randy Brown, a.k.a. "Charlie Sherpa"

Hugging This Rock:
Poems of Earth & Sky, Love & War
by Eric Chandler

www.ingramcontent.com/pod-product-compliance
Lightning Source LLC
Chambersburg PA
CBHW051837040426
42447CB00006B/568